THE ULTIMATE
SOUTHAMPTON FC
TRIVIA BOOK

A Collection of Amazing Trivia Quizzes
and Fun Facts for Die-Hard Saints Fans!

Ray Walker

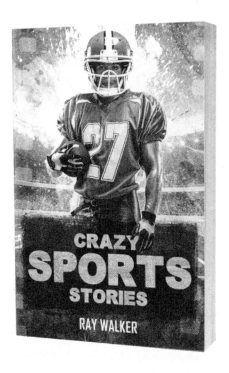

CONTENTS

INTRODUCTION

Starting out as a small church team in 1885, St. Mary's YMA evolved into Southampton FC and became one of the most popular soccer clubs in the UK. The team ruled the Southern League for several seasons before joining England's top league in 1920-21.

Nicknamed "The Saints" due to their ties with the church, the club won a division title in just its second season in the English Football League. The team eventually earned promotion to the top-tier and has spent most of its time there ever since.

Known for a tremendous never-say-die attitude and a large legion of passionate, loyal supporters, the Saints beat mighty Manchester United in 1975-76 to pull off one of the biggest upsets in English FA Cup history.

Southampton fans have had the pleasure and honor of following some of the world's best players in their iconic red and white kit at famous stadiums, The Dell and St. Mary's.

Who could ever forget the likes of skilled and colorful players and managers, such as Mick Channon, Alan Ball, Kevin Keegan, Peter Shilton, Cecil Knight, Ernest Arnfield, Ted Bates, Jimmy Case, Victor Wanyama, Ryan Bertrand, Lawrie

1

McMenemy, Tim Flowers, Adam Lallana, Maya Yoshida, Ivan Golac, Matt Le Tissier, Nathan Redmond, Alan Shearer, Martin Chivers, James Beattie, and Danny Wallace?

This trivia book has been published to help celebrate the wonderful history of Southampton FC from the club's humble beginnings right up to the 2020-21 Premier League campaign.

You'll read about the team's most famous characters and how each of them helped shape the club into what it is today.

The Saints' story is told here in quiz form, with 12 different chapters offering a unique trivia topic. Each chapter includes 20 enchanting quiz questions, along with 10 enthralling "Did You Know?" facts and anecdotes. The questions are divided into multiple-choice and true-false formats, and the answers are revealed on the following page.

This is the ideal way to challenge yourself on the intriguing history of Southampton FC and to jog your memory regarding the team's ups and downs. After absorbing all the information available, you'll be aching to test your knowledge by accepting trivia challenges from fellow fans.

CHAPTER 1:

ORIGINS & HISTORY

QUIZ TIME!

1. What year was the club founded?

   a. 1885

   b. 1888

   c. 1895

   d. 1901

2. Southampton was originally founded as St. Mary's Church of England Young Men's Association.

   a. True

   b. False

3. What was the first major league the team played in?

   a. The Football Alliance

   b. The Combination

   c. The Western Midland League

   d. The Southern League

4. What was St. Mary's original shirt color?

a. Yellow

b. Red and white

c. White

d. Black

5. What is the club's nickname?

    a. The Halos

    b. The Saints

    c. The Angels

    d. The Leathers

6. Against which team did the club play its first known game?

    a. Royal Engineers AFC

    b. Reading FC

    c. Freemantle FC

    d. Warmley FC

7. Southampton was a founding member of the Southern League.

    a. True

    b. False

8. How many games did the team win in its first Southern League season?

    a. 7

    b. 9

    c. 12

    d. 15

9. In which season did Southampton join the English Football League?

    a. 1946-47

    b. 1931-32

    c. 1920-21

    d. 1909-10

10. How many times has Southampton been relegated as of 2020?

    a. 6

    b. 8

    c. 2

    d. 4

11. The squad played its first Southern League match against which club?

    a. Luton Town FC

    b. Ilford FC

    c. Chatham Town FC

    d. Millwall Athletic

12. The team shared a stadium with Eastleigh FC between 1900 and 1903.

    a. True

    b. False

13. What was the outcome of the team's first Southern League match?

    a. 3-1 win

    b. 2-2 draw

c. 4-0 loss

d. 2-0 win

14. Against which club did Southampton play its first game in the Premier League?

    a. Tottenham Hotspur

    b. Queens Park Rangers

    c. Manchester United

    d. Aston Villa

15. What was the club's original crest design?

    a. A cross and a soccer ball

    b. Winchester cathedral

    c. A rose in a soccer ball

    d. Southampton city's coat of arms

16. The club was first relegated in 1959-60.

    a. True

    b. False

17. Which side did Southampton defeat to win its first Premier League match?

    a. Oldham Athletic

    b. Crystal Palace FC

    c. Manchester City FC

    d. Middlesbrough FC

18. How many games did Southampton win in its first season in the English Football League?

    a. 11

    b. 16

c. 19

d. 23

19. Which player scored the club's first goal in the Premier League?

    a. Kerry Dixon

    b. Matt Le Tissier

    c. Nicky Banger

    d. Michael Adams

20. The club officially changed its name to "Southampton FC" in 1888-89.

    a. True

    b. False

QUIZ ANSWERS

1. A – 1885

2. A – True

3. D – The Southern League

4. B – Red and white

5. B – The Saints

6. C – Freemantle FC

7. A – True

8. B – 9

9. C – 1920-21

10. D – 4

11. C – Chatham Town FC

12. B – False

13. A – 3-1 win

14. A – Tottenham Hotspur

15. D – Southampton city's coat of arms

16. B – False

17. D – Middlesbrough FC

18. C – 19

19. B – Matt Le Tissier

20. B – False

DID YOU KNOW?

1. The Southampton Football Club plays in the top-tier English Premier League and goes by the nickname the "Saints." The team's home games are hosted at St. Mary's Stadium in Southampton with a capacity of 32,384. The club's chairman is Gao Jisheng.

2. The side is nicknamed the Saints because of its roots as a church soccer team. When the club was founded, it was officially known as St. Mary's Church of England Young Men's Association, and the team colors were red and white shirts.

3. The club was originally founded in November 1885 and was commonly known as St. Mary's YMA. The club was a founding member of the Premier League and has spent most of its time in the top-flight since first earning promotion in 1966. The team's longest continuous period in the top-flight was for 27 seasons between 1978 and 2005.

4. The team's first known game took place on a pitch at the Hampshire County Cricket Club's new venue at Banister Court, a 5-1 victory over Freemantle. Ned Bromley scored three goals for the Saints while captain A.A. Fry netted two. The match took place shortly after the club was formed in November 1885.

5. Most of the team's early matches were held at the Southampton Common. However, since it was public

land, pedestrians often interrupted the action. More important contests such as cup games were held at the County Cricket Ground in Northlands Road or the Antelope Cricket Ground in St. Mary's Road.

6. In 1887-88, the club became known as St. Mary's FC and joined the Hampshire FA. The Saints won the Hampshire FA Junior Cup in 1890-91 and then captured the Hampshire FA Senior Cup in 1891-92 and 1892-93.

7. The Saints entered the FA Cup for the first time in 1891-92, beating Warmley 4-1 away and Reading 7-0 at home. However, Reading protested the result by claiming the Saints fielded two illegal players. The protest was upheld by the Football Association, and the team was eliminated from the competition that season.

8. The club became known as Southampton St. Mary's when it joined the country's Southern League in 1894. It then became a limited company in 1896-97 and was renamed Southampton FC. The team won the Southern League title three straight seasons from 1896-97 through 1898-99 and again in 1900-01, 1902-03, and 1903-04. It also moved to a newly built stadium called The Dell in 1898 and played there for the next 103 years, paying rent until being able to afford to buy the venue early in the twentieth century.

9. The squad reached its first FA Cup final in 1899-1900 but lost 4-0 to Bury and was then beaten by Sheffield United two years later. However, Southampton had now become known internationally, and, in 1909, Spanish soccer

officials visited the city and bought 50 of the team's shirts. They were shared between Atlético Madrid and Athletic Bilbao, and both those teams decided to wear red and white stripes.

10. After World War I, Southampton was elected to the newly formed Third Division of the English Football League in 1920, with the division splitting into South and North sections a year later. The club earned promotion following the 1921-22 campaign by topping their division and played in the Second Division for the next 31 years.

CHAPTER 2:

THE CAPTAIN CLASS

QUIZ TIME!

1. Who captained the club to its first Southern League title?

    a. Archie Turner
    b. Alf Littlehales
    c. John "Jack" Farrell
    d. George Carter

2. Charlie Baker captained the Saints in their inaugural Football League season.

    a. True
    b. False

3. Alan Ball captained which club before joining the Saints?

    a. Vancouver Whitecaps
    b. Bristol Rovers FC
    c. Portsmouth FC
    d. Arsenal FC

4. Adam Lallana left the Saints to join what club?

a. Manchester United

b. Chelsea FC

c. Tottenham Hotspur

d. Liverpool FC

5. Who captained Southampton during its first FA Cup final victory?

a. Harry Wood

b. Bobby Stokes

c. Peter Rodrigues

d. Bill Rawlings

6. Why did Charles Edward Bromley step down as the Saints' skipper?

a. To play hockey

b. To take over his father's butcher shop

c. To study dentistry

d. To study medicine

7. The Saints have never given the captain's armband to a goalkeeper.

a. True

b. False

8. Whom did James Ward-Prowse replace as captain?

a. Pierre-Emile Højbjerg

b. Nathan Redmond

c. Stuart Armstrong

d. José Fonte

9. Which club did Dean Richards captain before he joined the Saints?

   a. Tottenham Hotspur
   b. Stoke City FC
   c. Newcastle United
   d. Wolverhampton Wanderers

10. Which player took the captain's armband in place of Jason Dodd in the 2003 FA Cup final?

   a. Matt Oakley
   b. Anders Svensson
   c. Chris Marsden
   d. Antti Niemi

11. Which historic feat did former Saints goalkeeper Dave Beasant accomplish while with Wimbledon?

   a. First keeper to captain the English men's national team
   b. First keeper to captain a team to an FA Cup victory since 1875
   c. Youngest captain in Football League history
   d. Oldest captain in Football League history

12. Steven Davis became the youngest captain of the Northern Ireland men's national team as of 2020.

   a. True
   b. False

13. Which club did Dean Hammond skipper before joining Southampton?

a. Sheffield United

b. Worthing FC

c. Leicester City FC

d. Colchester United

14. James Ward-Prowse captained England's Under-21 squad in what 2016 competition?

a. Toulon Tournament

b. UEFA European Under-21 Championship

c. FIFA Under-21 World Cup

d. FIFA Youth Cup

15. Which player did Jason Dodd succeed as captain?

a. Dean Richards

b. Uwe Rösler

c. Matt Le Tissier

d. Matt Oakley

16. Southampton rotated the captaincy each month in the 2015-16 season.

a. True

b. False

17. Which club did Matt Oakley captain after he left the Saints?

a. Everton FC

b. Derby County FC

c. Preston North End

d. Bristol Rovers FC

18. Which player took the captaincy following Adam Lallana's departure?

    a. José Fonte

    b. Morgan Schneiderlin

    c. Dušan Tadić

    d. Victor Wanyama

19. Which club did Matt Le Tissier leave Southampton for?

    a. Leeds United

    b. Swindon Town FC

    c. Portsmouth FC

    d. Eastleigh FC

20. David Hughes was the Saints' first captain in the Premier League era.

    a. True

    b. False

QUIZ ANSWERS

1. C – John "Jack" Farrell

2. B – False

3. D – Arsenal FC

4. D – Liverpool FC

5. C – Peter Rodrigues

6. C – To study dentistry

7. B – False

8. A – Pierre-Emile Højbjerg

9. D – Wolverhampton Wanderers

10. C – Chris Marsden

11. B – First keeper to captain a team to an FA Cup victory since 1875

12. A – True

13. D – Colchester United

14. A – Toulon Tournament

15. C – Matt Le Tissier

16. B – False

17. B – Derby County FC

18. A – José Fonte

19. D – Eastleigh FC

20. B – False

DID YOU KNOW?

1. John "Jack" Farrell signed with Southampton St. Mary's in 1895 from Stoke City before the previous season had ended. Stoke complained, and the Saints were fined for "poaching" players. The center-forward led the team with 14 goals in his first season and 13 more in 1896-97 to help the team win the Southern League for the first time with an undefeated season. The skipper led the squad to the 1897-98 FA Cup semifinals and to a second straight Southern League crown. Farrell returned to Stoke in 1898 but was back with the Saints just a year later and helped the team reach the 1899-1900 FA Cup final. He scored 57 goals in 116 games before joining New Brighton Tower in 1900.

2. Portuguese international José Fonte signed in January 2010 from Crystal Palace for a reported fee of £1.2 million. He scored seven league goals that season, helping the club earn promotion to the second-tier by finishing as runner-up in League One. He was named to the PFA League One Team of the Year and was also named the Southampton Player of the Year for the 2010-11 season. He won that award again in 2014-15. In 2011-12, Fonte played 42 matches and helped the side earn a second consecutive promotion by finishing second in the Championship League. He was named captain in 2014 and joined West

Ham United in January 2017 for a reported £8 million. Fonte played 288 times with the Saints and contributed 15 goals.

3. After spending his youth with AFC Bournemouth, Adam Lallana joined the Southampton academy in 2000 and made his senior debut in 2006. He then returned to Bournemouth on loan for a spell in 2007. Lallana helped the side win the Football League Trophy in 2009-10, thus earning promotion from the third to the first tier by finishing as runner-up in League One in 2010-11 and the Championship League the following season. He was named skipper in 2012 and the team's Player of the Year for 2013-14. The English international midfielder was then sold to Liverpool for £27.9 million in July 2014 after 60 goals and 265 appearances with the club and was with Brighton & Hove Albion in 2020-21.

4. Known for his thunderous shot, midfielder Jimmy Case ended his career with numerous team medals including three European Cups and four top-tier league titles. Unfortunately, they were all won with Liverpool, where he kicked off his pro career from 1973 to 1981. He then played with Brighton & Hove Albion before joining the Saints in March 1985 for a reported £30,000. Case was appointed skipper by manager Chris Nicholl and was voted the team's Player of the Year for 1988-89. When Ian Branfoot took over as manager, Case was sold to AFC Bournemouth in 1991 after 272 matches and 14 goals with the club.

5. Midfielder Chris Marsden was 30 years old when he arrived at Southampton from Birmingham City in 1999 for a reported £800,000 and went on to score eight goals in 152 contests before heading to South Korea to play in 2004. He eventually ended his career a year later with Sheffield Wednesday after appearing in over 425 career league contests. Marsden helped the Saints reach the 2002-03 FA Cup final and wore the captain's armband for the match at the Millennium Stadium in Cardiff, Wales, which they lost to Arsenal.

6. After helping England win the 1966 World Cup, Alan Ball enjoyed two stints with Southampton as a player and later managed the club. He first arrived in 1976 from Arsenal and helped the side earn promotion to the top-flight by finishing in second place in the Second Division in 1977-78. The team also reached the League Cup final in 1978-79 with Ball as skipper. He left to play in North America but rejoined the Saints from Blackpool from March 1981 to October 1982 before joining Eastern Athletic in Hong Kong. Ball scored 13 goals in 234 outings for the team and later managed the side between 1994 and 1995.

7. Starting with Southampton as an apprentice, Steve Williams then played with the senior side from 1976 to 1984 while making his debut at the age of 17. He was voted the team's Player of the Year for 1976-77, helped the side reach the League Cup final in 1978-79, and took over the captain's armband from Alan Ball. Williams helped the team finish First Division runner-up in 1983-84 and

then joined Arsenal in December 1984 for what was then a record £550,000 transfer fee for the Saints. Williams left with 27 goals to his name for the club in 349 appearances, and he also played six times for England.

8. Goalkeeper Kelvin Davis spent a decade at The Dell after arriving in 2006 from Sunderland and played 301 games. He skippered the side from 2009 to 2012 before retiring in 2016. He remained with the club to work with the support staff and then became the senior first-team coach. He also took over as caretaker manager for a brief spell in December 2018 when Mark Hughes was fired. While playing, Davis helped the team win the Football League Trophy in 2009-10 and finish as runner-up in League One in 2010-11 and the Championship League in 2011-12. He was voted the team's Player of the Season for 2008-09 and was named to three PFA Teams of the Year while with the club.

9. Born in Southampton, Nick Holmes joined as an apprentice and debuted with the first-team in 1974. He spent his entire pro career with the team until 1987, appearing in 543 games and scoring 64 goals. He won the 1975-76 FA Cup and scored in the 1978-79 League Cup final defeat by Nottingham Forest. Holmes also helped the team finish second in the Second Division in 1977-78 to earn promotion back to the top-flight. Holmes was given the captain's armband in 1980 and led the side to the runner-up spot in the First Division in 1983-84. He retired due to an injury and is currently ranked number

three on the Saints' all-time appearance list. He later spent time as a coach at The Dell, working with manager Chris Nicholl before moving to America.

10. Although he was just 26 years old in April 2021, central midfielder James Ward-Prowse had already played over 300 games with the Saints and was the club captain. The English international was originally a member of the club's youth system and made his senior debut in October 2011. He was appointed skipper in June 2020, replacing Pierre-Emile Højbjerg, and has represented England at the under-17, under-19, under-20, and under-21 levels and had played six times for the senior national team. Ward-Prowse can also play right-back if needed and has contributed over 30 goals.

CHAPTER 3:

AMAZING MANAGERS

QUIZ TIME!

1. Who was the club's first known secretary-manager?

   a. Ernest Arnfield
   b. Cecil Knight
   c. George Robson
   d. Alfred McMinn

2. The club was managed by a committee between 1890 and 1896.

   a. True
   b. False

3. Who is the Saints' most successful manager in terms of silverware won as of 2020?

   a. Ted Bates
   b. Jimmy McIntyre
   c. Ernest Arnfield
   d. Lawrie McMenemy

4. Who was Southampton's first known full-time manager?

    a. Bill Dodgin

    b. George Kay

    c. Arthur Chadwick

    d. George Swift

5. Nigel Adkins left what club to manage Southampton?

    a. Charlton Athletic

    b. Scunthorpe United

    c. Sheffield United

    d. Fulham FC

6. How many trophies did Lawrie McMenemy win with the club?

    a. 6

    b. 4

    c. 3

    d. 1

7. Ted Bates was nicknamed "Mr. Southampton."

    a. True

    b. False

8. Who managed the Saints to their first Southern League title?

    a. Alfred McMinn

    b. Jimmy McIntyre

    c. Tom Parker

    d. Sid Cann

9. Ronald Koeman left Southampton to manage which club?

   a. RCD Espanyol

   b. Ajax

   c. Everton FC

   d. Manchester City

10. Who managed Southampton in its first European competition?

    a. George Roughton

    b. Ted Bates

    c. Lawrie McMenemy

    d. Chris Nicholl

11. Who was the Saints' first manager in the Premier League?

    a. David Merrington

    b. Alan Ball

    c. Ian Branfoot

    d. Chris Nicholl

12. Ted Bates managed Southampton in over 800 matches.

    a. True

    b. False

13. Whom did Ralph Hasenhüttl succeed as manager?

    a. Mark Hughes

    b. Mauricio Pellegrino

    c. Claude Puel

    d. Ronald Koeman

14. How many Southern League titles did Ernest Arnfield win with the club?

    a. 3
    b. 5
    c. 7
    d. 8

15. From which club did Ralph Hasenhüttl join the Saints?

    a. PSV Eindhoven
    b. 1. FC Köln
    c. FC Red Bull Salzburg
    d. RB Leipzig

16. Charles Robson managed the team in its first FA Cup final.

    a. True
    b. False

17. Who was Southampton's first manager born outside of the British Isles?

    a. Claude Puel
    b. Ronald Koeman
    c. Mauricio Pochettino
    d. Jan Poortvliet

18. Which club did George Burley manage after leaving Southampton?

    a. Preston North End
    b. Newcastle United

c. Coventry City FC

d. Crystal Palace FC

19. Whom did Gordon Strachan replace as manager?

    a. Steve Wigley

    b. Dave Jones

    c. Stuart Gray

    d. Glenn Hoddle

20. Jimmy McIntyre managed the Saints in their first season in the Football League.

    a. True

    b. False

QUIZ ANSWERS

1. B – Cecil Knight

2. B – False

3. C – Ernest Arnfield

4. D – George Swift

5. B – Scunthorpe United

6. D – 1

7. A – True

8. A – Alfred McMinn

9. C – Everton FC

10. B – Ted Bates

11. C – Ian Branfoot

12. A – True

13. A – Mark Hughes

14. B – 5

15. D – RB Leipzig

16. B – False

17. D – Jan Poortvliet

18. D – Crystal Palace FC

19. C – Stuart Gray

20. A – True

DID YOU KNOW?

1. Southampton has employed approximately 48 full-time and caretaker managers and secretary-managers from the club's formation in 1885 to 2021. The first known secretary-manager of the club was Cecil Knight from 1892 to 1895, and the first known full-time manager was George Swift from 1911 to 1912. The manager as of April 2021 was Ralph Hasenhüttl of Austria, who was appointed in December 2018.

2. When it comes to winning silverware with the Saints, the most successful manager was Ernest Arnfield of England. He was in charge of the club from August 1912 to May 1919 and won the Southern Football League five times and the Western Football League Division 1A once. He was in charge for more than 500 games and also guided the side to the FA Cup final in 1899-1900 and 1901-02.

3. The longest-serving manager with Southampton has been Ted Bates of England. The former Saints player held the job between 1955 and 1973. Bates was in charge for approximately 850 official matches and was nicknamed "Mr. Southampton." He led the team to the third-tier Third Division championship in 1959-60 and was the first manager of the team in European competition.

4. All but seven of Southampton's full-time managers have hailed from Great Britain (England, Scotland, Wales, and

Northern Ireland). Jan Poortvliet (2008-09), Mark Wotte (2009), and Ronald Koeman (2014-16) were Dutch, while Mauricio Pochettino (2013-14) and Mauricio Pellegrino (2017-18) hailed from Argentina. Claude Puel (2016-17) was French, and current boss Ralph Hasenhüttl is Austrian.

5. The first non-British boss was Jan Poortvliet of Holland. The former international defender was announced as the Saints' boss in May 2008 to replace Nigel Pearson, while fellow Dutchman Mark Wotte took over the academy teams. Poortvliet was the side's tenth manager in 10 years, but Southampton found out he was still under contract to Helmond Sport for another year. Poortvliet offered to buy his way out of his existing contract for €30,000. The Dutch club rejected his offer, and the situation was resolved by an arbitration panel, with the manager being required to pay Helmond Sport €75,000. After only one victory in 14 home outings, he resigned in January 2009 and was replaced by Poortvliet and Wotte.

6. Alfred McMinn of England was the first manager to win the Southern League title, in 1896-97. Before being appointed manager, he was a club committee member who helped recruit players along with Charles Robson. The problem was that some of the players were already members of other clubs, and Southampton was fined by the Football Association for "poaching." The club was ordered to pay compensation to both Stoke City and Port Vale, and McMinn was suspended for a year. He took over as the club's manager following the suspension but

stepped down after one season. He became the honorary secretary of the newly formed Southampton Football & Athletic Company Limited from 1897 to 1900.

7. It didn't take Southampton long to win a title after entering the Football League in 1920-21, as they hoisted the Third Division South championship in 1921-22 under manager Jimmy McIntyre of England. The former player arrived at the club in 1912 as a trainer but left for Coventry to work in a munitions factory during World War I. He returned to The Dell in 1919 as the manager when league soccer resumed. The club was admitted into the third tier of the Football League in 1920 and won the title the following season by goal difference over Plymouth Argyle. The Saints conceded just 21 goals in 42 league games that season to set a Football League record that stood until 1979. In December 1924, McIntyre resigned as manager and moved to Scotland to run a hotel.

8. The only Southampton manager to win the FA Cup was Lawrie McMenemy of England. He was hired as assistant manager in the summer of 1973 and promoted to manager in November 1973. However, the side was relegated to the Second Division following the season. While still in the second tier, he led his experienced team to its famous 1-0 victory over Manchester United in the 1975-76 FA Cup final. The club earned promotion to the top-tier after finishing Second Division runner-up in 1977-78 and reached the League Cup final in 1978-79 under McMenemy. He then led the team to second place in the

First Division in 1983-84 before joining Sunderland in June 1985.

9. The club's longest-serving manager since 1985 has been Chris Nicholl, who held the job from July 1985 to May 1991. The English-born Northern Ireland international defender played with the Saints between 1977 and 1983, appearing in 268 games and chipping in with eight goals. After serving Grimsby Town as assistant manager, he was named Southampton boss when Lawrie McMenemy resigned. His best season with the team saw them finish in seventh place in the First Division in 1989-90. After the side placed 14th in 1990-91, he was fired and Ian Branfoot took over. The club had just three managers in the previous 36 years, and then appointed 12 bosses in the next 15 years.

10. The last piece of silverware won by the Saints was the Football League Trophy in 2009-10, with Alan Pardew of England as manager. Pardew was named the boss in July 2009 after new owner Markus Liebherr fired Mark Wotte. Pardew signed players such as strikers Rickie Lambert and Lee Barnard, and even though his side had 10 points deducted to begin the season, the team challenged for a second-tier playoff spot until the final two games of the campaign. The squad won the League Trophy for their first silverware since the FA Cup in 1975-76. Pardew posted one of the club's best winning percentages at 53.13 but was fired just over a year after taking over.

CHAPTER 4:

GOALTENDING GREATS

QUIZ TIME!

1. Which keeper made the most appearances for Southampton in all competitions?

   a. George Clawley

   b. Eric Martin

   c. Kelvin Davis

   d. Tommy Allen

2. Tim Flowers played in the Saints' very first Premier League match.

   a. True

   b. False

3. How many clean sheets did Kelvin Davis keep in the 2010-11 domestic league?

   a. 14

   b. 17

   c. 20

   d. 24

4. Which club did Alex McCarthy leave to join Southampton?

    a. Watford FC
    b. Middlesbrough FC
    c. Crystal Palace FC
    d. Leyton Orient FC

5. Which keeper made 18 appearances in the 1997-98 domestic league?

    a. Bruce Grobbelaar
    b. Maik Taylor
    c. Dave Beasant
    d. Chris Woods

6. Who backed up Antti Niemi in 14 matches in the 2003-04 Premier League season?

    a. Paul Jones
    b. Alan Blayney
    c. Kasey Keller
    d. Neil Moss

7. Tim Flowers appeared in every match in the 1992-93 Premier League.

    a. True
    b. False

8. How many clean sheets did Artur Boruc keep in the 2013-14 domestic league?

    a. 17
    b. 14

c. 10

d. 7

9. From which club did Dave Beasant join Southampton?

    a. Tottenham Hotspur

    b. Chelsea FC

    c. Manchester City FC

    d. Brighton & Hove Albion

10. How many appearances did Eric Martin make in all competitions?

    a. 247

    b. 263

    c. 290

    d. 325

11. Who backed up Alex McCarthy in 12 matches in the 2018-19 domestic league?

    a. Maarten Strekelenburg

    b. Paulo Gazzaniga

    c. Fraser Forster

    d. Angus Gunn

12. Tim Flowers made 15 appearances for the English men's national team while playing for Southampton.

    a. True

    b. False

13. Which keeper enjoyed two stints with the club?

    a. George Clawley

    b. Eric Martin

c. Paul Jones

d. Peter Wells

14. How many appearances in all competitions did Kelvin Davis make for the Saints?

   a. 346

   b. 317

   c. 301

   d. 278

15. Who appeared in 30 matches in the 1994-95 Premier League?

   a. John Burridge

   b. Ian Andrews

   c. Chris Woods

   d. Bruce Grobbelaar

16. Paul Jones was capped 50 times by the Welsh men's national team.

   a. True

   b. False

17. How many appearances did Tommy Allen make in all competitions for the Saints?

   a. 364

   b. 327

   c. 285

   d. 264

18. Who made seven appearances behind Kelvin Davis in the 2009-10 domestic league season?

a. Bartosz Bialkowski

b. Richard Wright

c. Paulo Gazzaniga

d. Artur Boruc

19. How many appearances did Alex McCarthy make in the 2019-20 domestic league?

   a. 19

   b. 25

   c. 28

   d. 33

20. Tony Godfrey made four appearances for the English men's national team.

   a. True

   b. False

QUIZ ANSWERS

1. D – Tommy Allen

2. A – True

3. C – 20

4. C – Crystal Palace FC

5. B – Maik Taylor

6. A – Paul Jones

7. A – True

8. B – 14

9. B – Chelsea FC

10. C – 290

11. D – Angus Gunn

12. B – False

13. A – George Clawley

14. C – 301

15. D – Bruce Grobbelaar

16. A – True

17. B – 327

18. A – Bartosz Bialkowski

19. C – 28

20. B – False

DID YOU KNOW?

1. Saints goalkeepers who have been honored with the fans' Player of the Year Award are: 1984-85, Peter Shilton; 1985-86, Peter Shilton; 1991-92, Tim Flowers; 1992-93, Tim Flowers; 1995-96, Dave Beasant; 1997-98, Paul Jones; 2003-04, Antti Niemi; 2008-09, Kelvin Davis; and 2017-18, Alex McCarthy.

2. When it comes to making appearances for the club, the top 10 keepers in Southampton history are: Tommy Allen, 327 (1920-28); Kelvin Davis, 301 (2006-16); Eric Martin, 290 (1967-75); George Clawley, 267 (1896-98 and 1903-07); Tim Flowers, 251 (1986-93); Peter Shilton, 242 (1982-87); Bert Scriven, 241 (1930-37); Paul Jones, 223 (1997-2003); John Christie, 217 (1951-59); and John "Jack" Robinson, 201 (1898-1903).

3. John "Jack" Robinson was 28 years old and had already played 163 times for Derby County when he arrived at Southampton in 1898. He helped the club win three Southern League titles and runner-up medals in the 1899-1900 and 1901-02 FA Cup finals. He was the first Saints player to be capped for England and the first keeper to reach double figures in appearances for his homeland. Robinson played 201 contests for Southampton before joining Plymouth Argyle in 1903. He finished his career in Rochester, New York. Robinson also played professional

baseball for the Derby Baseball Club in the National League of Baseball of Great Britain in the 1890s.

4. With 327 appearances, Tommy Allen played more games for the club than any other keeper. He arrived in 1920 from Sunderland when Southampton was elected to the English Football League. He posted 26 clean sheets in 1921-22 to help the team capture the Third Division South title on goal average over Plymouth Argyle. Allen didn't allow a goal in the final seven games of the season and at one point went 845 minutes without conceding a goal. Allen was well known for his excellent play in FA Cup games and helped the side reach the semifinals in the competition on a few occasions. He joined Coventry City in 1928 and hung up his boots a decade later.

5. English international and Football Hall of Fame member Peter Shilton was a legendary keeper for club and country and currently holds the record for appearances with the national senior side at 125. He also played in 1,390 competitive games during his career, which is considered a world record for a soccer player. Shilton's pro career lasted from 1966 to 1997, with 11 different clubs. He won numerous team and individual awards, most of them with Nottingham Forest. He arrived at The Dell from Forest in 1982 and played 242 times, helping the side finish as First Division runner-up in 1983-84. Shilton was named the team's Player of the Year for 1984-85 and 1985-86 before joining Derby County in 1987.

6. In 1986, English international Tim Flowers joined First Division Southampton for a reported £70,000 from Wolverhampton Wanderers to back up Peter Shilton. He played just nine league games in his first season and was also loaned to third-tier club Swindon Town. When Shilton left the club in 1987, Flowers gradually took over the number-one position between the posts. The club's Player of the Year for 1991-92 and 1992-93, he played 251 times with the squad before joining Blackburn Rovers for £2.4 million in November 1993, making him the most expensive keeper in Britain. Flowers went on to win the Premier League with Blackburn and the League Cup with Leicester City.

7. Dave Beasant played with well over a dozen clubs during his career between the posts with a stint at Southampton from 1993 to 1997. He arrived from Chelsea in November 1993 for a fee of £300,000 to replace the recently departed Tim Flowers. Beasant quickly became a fan favorite and was named their Player of the Year for 1995-96. He suffered injuries the next season and soon found himself the third-choice keeper after Paul Jones arrived in the summer of 1997. Beasant was loaned to Nottingham Forest in August 1997 and signed permanently with the club in November after 105 appearances with the Saints.

8. Welsh international Paul Jones played 50 games for his country and 223 times for Southampton. When former Stockport County manager Dave Jones took over as boss at The Dell, he signed Jones from his previous club. It didn't

take the keeper long to get used to his new surroundings, as he was the Saints' Player of the Year for 1997-98. He played in the 2002-03 FA Cup final defeat to Arsenal when starting keeper Antti Niemi suffered an injury, making him the first keeper ever to play as a substitute in an FA Cup final. Jones was loaned to Liverpool in 2004 and signed with Wolverhampton Wanderers shortly afterward.

9. After playing in Finland, Denmark, and Scotland, Finnish international Antti Niemi joined Southampton in 2002 from Heart of Midlothian. He helped the side reach the 2002-03 FA Cup final but had to leave the game due to a calf injury. The club was relegated after the 2004-05 campaign, and Niemi decided to return to the Premier League with Fulham in January 2006. He was named the Saints' Player of the Year for 2003-04 and played 123 games with the team while appearing in 67 outings for Finland.

10. On August 1, 2016, Alex McCarthy joined the Saints from Crystal Palace and signed a three-year contract. He was initially used as the backup to Fraser Forster but eventually took over the top job. He was named the club's Player of the Year for 2017-18 and signed a new four-year deal in June 2018. However, he found himself number two in the pecking order behind Angus Gunn early in 2019-20 but soon regained his place as the number-one keeper. McCarthy tested positive for COVID-19 in January 2021 but soon recovered. He was still with the club as of April 2021 and had made just over 100 career appearances for the side.

CHAPTER 5:

DARING DEFENDERS

QUIZ TIME!

1. Who played the most matches with the club?

    a. Claus Lundekvam

    b. Jason Dodd

    c. Francis Benali

    d. Tommy Traynor

2. Ken Monkou was shown 10 yellow cards in the 1994-95 domestic league season.

    a. True

    b. False

3. Who scored two goals in the 2012-13 Premier League?

    a. Danny Fox

    b. José Fonte

    c. Jos Hooiveld

    d. Maya Yoshida

4. Which player appeared in 29 matches in all competitions in 2018-19?

a. Jan Bednarek

b. Ryan Bertrand

c. Jack Stephens

d. Matt Target

5. How many goals did Chris Perry notch in the 2008-09 Championship League?

a. 2

b. 4

c. 5

d. 7

6. Which player tallied five assists in the 2016-17 Premier League?

a. Cuco Martina

b. Martín Cáceres

c. Maya Yoshida

d. Ryan Bertrand

7. Tahar El Khalej was the only Saints player shown a red card in the 2000-01 domestic league.

a. True

b. False

8. Which club did Jason Dodd leave to join the Saints?

a. Bath City FC

b. Aldershot Town FC

c. Stoke City FC

d. Wimbledon FC

9. How many appearances did Claus Lundekvam make in all competitions for Southampton?

   a. 452
   b. 413
   c. 398
   d. 374

10. Who scored seven goals in the 2011-12 domestic league?

   a. Dan Harding
   b. José Fonte
   c. Jos Hooiveld
   d. Aaron Martin

11. How many goals did Virgil van Dijk score in all competitions in 2015-16?

   a. 8
   b. 5
   c. 3
   d. 1

12. Claus Lundekvam was capped 40 times by the Norwegian men's national team.

   a. True
   b. False

13. Who appeared in 49 matches in all competitions in 2009-10?

   a. Joseph Mills
   b. Wayne Thomas

    c. Radhi Jaidi

    d. Dan Harding

14. Chris Nicholl joined the Saints from which club?

    a. Chelsea FC

    b. Aston Villa

    c. Tottenham Hotspur

    d. West Ham United

15. How many appearances did Tommy Traynor make in all competitions?

    a. 425

    b. 466

    c. 487

    d. 514

16. Southampton was the only top-flight team Dennis Hollywood played for.

    a. True

    b. False

17. Which club did David Peach leave to join Southampton?

    a. Sunderland AFC

    b. Newcastle United

    c. Swindon Town FC

    d. Gillingham FC

18. How many appearances did Jason Dodd make for the Saints in all competitions?

    a. 509

    b. 483

c. 445

d. 417

19. Which player appeared in 41 games in the 1993-94 Premier League?

a. Francis Benali

b. Wayne Bridge

c. Dean Richards

d. Jeff Kenna

20. Francis Benali scored only one goal in 369 games with the Saints.

a. True

b. False

QUIZ ANSWERS

1. D – Tommy Traynor

2. B – False

3. B – José Fonte

4. C – Jack Stephens

5. A – 2

6. D – Ryan Bertrand

7. B – False

8. A – Bath City FC

9. B – 413

10. C – Jos Hooiveld

11. C – 3

12. A – True

13. D – Dan Harding

14. B – Aston Villa

15. C – 487

16. A – True

17. D – Gillingham FC

18. B – 483

19. D – Jeff Kenna

20. A – True

DID YOU KNOW?

1. The following defenders have received the fans' Player of the Year award: 1974-75, Mel Blyth; 1975-76, David Peach; 1978-79, Malcolm Waldron; 1980-81, Ivan Golac; 1982-83, Mark Wright; 1987-88, Derek Statham; 1999-2000, Dean Richards; 2000-01, Wayne Bridge; 2005-06, Claus Lundekvam; 2006-07, Chris Baird; 2007-08, Andrew Davies; 2010-11, José Fonte; and 2014-15, José Fonte.

2. Republic of Ireland international Thomas "Tommy" Traynor played his entire pro career in England for Southampton from 1952 to 1966 after arriving from Dundalk in his homeland. He played 487 games for the team, which was a club record when he retired. He reportedly turned down offers from Chelsea and Manchester City to join the Saints and became the side's regular left-back. He was relegated with the team but helped them earn promotion by winning the Third Division in 1959-60. Traynor was a founding member of the Southampton Tyro League in the late 1960s and also worked on the Southampton Docks after his playing days.

3. The unheralded Jason Dodd made 483 outings with Southampton and chipped in with 13 goals between 1989 and 2005. He joined from Bath City and spent part of 2004 on loan with Plymouth Argyle before signing with Brighton & Hove Albion a year later. He also acted as

caretaker manager for the Saints in 2008 alongside John Gorman for a brief time. As director of the youth academy, he helped develop players such as Luke Shaw, Calum Chambers, and James Ward-Prowse.

4. English-born Nigerian international Reuben Omojola Folasanje Agboola began his career as an amateur with Southampton in 1978 and played 112 times with the first team from 1980 to 1985 before joining Sunderland for a reported £150,000. He helped the Saints reach the FA Cup semifinals in 1983-84 and finish second in the First Division. He was a part-time player during his first two seasons, but in November 1982, he started playing regularly and formed a fine partnership with Mick Mills. Agboola played nine times with Nigeria, later ran a pub in Southampton, and moved to Majorca to run a bar in 2004.

5. Frederick "Bert" Shelley played soccer in the military while serving in India and Egypt during World War I and joined Southampton shortly after the war in 1919. The club entered the English Football League in 1920-21 and won the Third Division South a year later after finishing as runner-up in their first campaign. Shelley played in 465 career games with the club to set the appearance record at the time. After hanging up his boots, he remained at The Dell to help coach the club's youngsters in the Hampshire League.

6. Claus Lundekvam was a Norwegian international who began his career with Brann in his homeland before

joining Southampton in 1996 and playing with the team until retiring in 2008 due to injury. He appeared in 413 games and helped the side reach the 2002-03 FA Cup final against Arsenal. Lundekvam also played 40 times for Norway and often wore the captain's armband. He was named the Saints' Player of the Year for 2005-06 but suffered from addiction problems for a time after retiring. He then became a television pundit before helping others with mental health and drug problems.

7. English international Ryan Bertrand arrived at The Dell on loan from Chelsea in July 2014 and signed permanently in February 2015. He signed a 4.5-year contract and was named to the PFA Premier League Team of the Year for 2014-15. He then signed a new five-year contract in July 2016 and was still with the club at the age of 31 in April 2021, having appeared in over 230 games. Bertrand has played for England 19 times and also represented the country at five other levels and played for Great Britain at the 2012 Olympics.

8. When English international Mark Wright arrived at The Dell from Oxford United in March 1982, he was just 18 years old. He notched two goals in 39 appearances in 1982-83 and was voted the Player of the Year by the Saints' fans. He helped the side finish second place in the First Division in 1983-84 as they ended up three points back of Liverpool. Wright's play at the heart of the team's defense that season led to his England debut in May 1984, and he went on to play 45 times for his country. He

appeared 222 times for Southampton, scoring 11 goals, before joining Derby County for what was then a club-record fee of £760,000 in 1987. He later became a soccer manager and television pundit.

9. Maya Yoshida started his career in his homeland of Japan before joining Dutch outfit VVV-Venlo. He signed with Southampton in August 2012 after the team was promoted back to the Premier League. He quickly became a first-team center-back in tandem with José Fonte. However, he moved down and up the pecking order over the next several seasons before being loaned to Sampdoria of Italy in January 2020 and then making the move permanent. Yoshida has played 106 games with Japan, often as captain, and represented his country at the 2012 Olympics. He played 194 times with the Saints and scored nine goals.

10. Born in the former nation of Yugoslavia, Ivan Golac joined the Saints in August 1978 from Partizan in his homeland as a 28-year-old. He moved to England after Yugoslavia's Communist regime began to allow players to move abroad and cost the club a £50,000 transfer fee. Golac was voted the club's Player of the Year for 1980-81. Following a contract dispute, he was loaned to AFC Bournemouth in November 1982 and Manchester City in March 1983. He soon returned to his homeland but rejoined Southampton in March 1984 and helped the side finish as runner-up in the First Division. Golac was loaned to Portsmouth for a spell in 1985 and hung up his boots a

year later after 197 games with the Saints to become a
soccer manager.

CHAPTER 6:

MAESTROS OF THE MIDFIELD

QUIZ TIME!

1. Which player appeared in the most games with the team?

    a. Matt Le Tissier

    b. Nick Holmes

    c. Bert Shelley

    d. John Sydenham

2. Glenn Cockerill left Lincoln City FC to join the Saints.

    a. True

    b. False

3. How many goals did Dean Hammond score in the 2009-10 domestic league season?

    a. 5

    b. 7

    c. 10

    d. 12

4. Which player appeared in 46 matches in all competitions in 2016-17?

a. Pierre-Emile Højbjerg

b. Steven Davis

c. James Ward-Prowse

d. Oriol Romeu

5. Stuart Armstrong left which Scottish club to join Southampton?

a. Celtic FC

b. Motherwell FC

c. Aberdeen FC

d. Partick Thistle FC

6. How many goals did Matt Le Tissier score in the 1998-99 Premier League?

a. 2

b. 5

c. 7

d. 13

7. James Ward-Prowse was capped 31 times by England's Under-21 squad.

a. True

b. False

8. How many appearances did Bert Shelley make in all competitions with Southampton?

a. 526

b. 479

c. 465

d. 383

9. Which player notched four goals in the 2004-05 domestic league?

   a. Matt Oakley
   b. Rory Delap
   c. Anders Svensson
   d. David Prutton

10. How many appearances did Matt Le Tissier make in all competitions for the Saints?

   a. 558
   b. 540
   c. 521
   d. 460

11. Who scored four goals in the 2005-06 domestic league season?

   a. Nigel Quashie
   b. Djamel Belmadi
   c. Matt Oakley
   d. Andrew Surman

12. Pierre-Emile Højbjerg was the only Southampton player to be shown a red card in 2018-19.

   a. True
   b. False

13. Which player appeared in 45 games in all competitions in 2009-10?

   a. Lloyd James
   b. Dean Hammond

c. Morgan Schneiderlin

d. Paul Wotton

14. Steve Williams left Southampton for which team?

    a. Manchester City

    b. Sevilla FC

    c. New York Cosmos

    d. Arsenal FC

15. How many career appearances did Nick Holmes make with the team?

    a. 410

    b. 458

    c. 543

    d. 567

16. Matt Le Tissier was capped 10 times by the English men's national team.

    a. True

    b. False

17. Who scored five goals in all competitions in 2012-13?

    a. Steven Davis

    b. Morgan Schneiderlin

    c. Gastón Ramírez

    d. Jack Cork

18. How many goals did Samuel Meston score in his 413 matches in all competitions with the Saints?

    a. 41

    b. 15

c. 33

d. 27

19. Who scored five goals in the 2015-16 Premier League?

    a. Steven Davis

    b. James Ward-Prowse

    c. Oriol Romeu

    d. Victor Wanyama

20. Matt Oakley played in every Premier League match in 2000-01.

    a. True

    b. False

QUIZ ANSWERS

1. B – Nick Holmes

2. B – False

3. A – 5

4. D – Oriol Romeu

5. A – Celtic FC

6. C – 7

7. A – True

8. C – 465

9. C – Anders Svensson

10. B – 540

11. A – Nigel Quashie

12. A – True

13. B – Dean Hammond

14. D – Arsenal FC

15. C – 543

16. B – False

17. B – Morgan Schneiderlin

18. D – 27

19. A – Steven Davis

20. B – False

DID YOU KNOW?

1. The following Southampton midfielders were voted by the club's fans as the team's Player of the Year: 1976-77, Steve Williams; 1977-78, Alan Ball; 1983-84, David Armstrong; 1986-87, Glenn Cockerill; 1988-89, Jimmy Case; 1989-90, Matt Le Tissier; 1993-94, Matt Le Tissier; 1994-95, Matt Le Tissier; 2001-02, Chris Marsden; 2012-13, Morgan Schneiderlin; 2013-14, Adam Lallana; 2016-17, Oriol Romeu; 2018-19, Nathan Redmond.

2. French international Morgan Schneiderlin joined the Saints from Strasbourg in 2008 after turning down a chance to join rival Portsmouth. He ended up playing 261 games with the club while notching 15 goals. He helped the side rise from the third tier to the Premier League by finishing as League One runner-up in 2010-11 and Championship League runner-up in 2011-12. He also helped the squad hoist the Football League Trophy in 2009-10 and was voted the team's Player of the Year as well as the Players' Player of the Year for 2012-13. Schneiderlin was then sold to Manchester United in the summer of 2015.

3. David Armstrong arrived at The Dell in 1981 from Middlesbrough and tallied 15 league goals in his first season while playing alongside Kevin Keegan. He helped the side finish as First Division runner-up in 1983-84 and reach the final four in the FA Cup. Armstrong helped the

team reach another FA Cup semifinal in 1985-86 but saw his playing time reduced in 1986-87. Following the season, he joined AFC Bournemouth in the second tier and hung up his boots a year later. Armstrong was voted the club's Player of the Year for 1983-84 and netted 71 goals in his 272 outings with the squad.

4. Nathan Redmond arrived in Southampton from Norwich City in June 2016, helping the side reach the League Cup final that season. He was still with the club in April 2021 with close to 200 games and 30 goals under his belt. He scored in his competitive debut and won the club's and the fans' Player of the Year awards for 2018-19. He then signed a new four-year deal that takes him to the summer of 2023. Redmond scored two goals in March 2021 in a 3-0 win over Bournemouth to help the side reach the FA Cup semifinals. He's represented England at seven different levels, including playing once for the senior national squad.

5. Also with the Saints in April 2021 was defensive midfielder Oriol Romeu of Spain with over 200 appearances for the squad. He joined in August 2015 from Chelsea for a reported £5 million and signed a three-year deal. He played 35 of 36 league games in 2016-17 and then signed a new 4.5-year contract in January 2017. The fans and club named him the 2016-17 Player of the Season, and he helped the team reach the League Cup final. Romeu required ankle surgery in February 2021 that sidelined him for the season.

6. Kenyan international captain Victor Wanyama was playing with MLS club Montreal in 2021, but before that, he was the first Kenyan to score in the UEFA Champions League while playing for Glasgow Celtic in 2012. He joined Southampton in July 2013 for a reported £12.5 million, making him the most expensive player sold by a Scottish club at the time and the first Kenyan to play in the Premier League. Wanyama appeared in 97 games and posted four goals before joining Tottenham Hotspur in June 2016 for a reported £11 million.

7. Jim Magilton was a Northern Ireland international who arrived from Oxford United midway through his career in 1994. He was the club's second signing under new manager Alan Ball and cost the club a reported £600,000. He quickly became one of the side's most dependable central midfielders and was a force at both ends of the pitch. He started all 42 league matches in 1994-95 and chipped in with six goals. Magilton joined Sheffield Wednesday in September 1997 for a reported £1.6 million after scoring 18 goals in 156 matches with the Saints.

8. Southampton was the fifth stop for Glenn Cockerill during his eight-club pro career. He arrived from Sheffield United in October 1985 and remained until joining Leyton Orient in December 1993. While at The Dell, he was voted the Player of the Year for 1986-87 and registered 39 goals in 358 matches. Cockerill's father Ron and brother John Cockerill were also pro soccer players. After hanging up his boots, Glenn tried his hand at soccer management with a couple

of semi-pro teams.

9. Walter Pollard was just 16 years old when he joined his hometown team, Burnley, in 1925. After playing just 20 official matches in four years he joined West Ham United, only to see the club relegated to the Second Division. Pollard tried his luck as a player-coach in France with Sochaux in 1933-34 and then signed with Fulham. He didn't get a game there, though, and joined Southampton in 1934. He contributed three goals in 24 official matches and helped coach the younger players before leaving for Brighton & Hove Albion in 1936. Pollard retired a year later and passed away from a heart attack in 1945 at the age of 38.

10. Mark Walters played nearly 750 career club games and scored 167 goals during his 20-year career but played just nine of them with Southampton. He had already made a name for himself with Aston Villa, Glasgow Rangers, and Liverpool and helped each club win articles of silverware. He was signed for the Saints by manager David Merrington in January 1996 to help the side avoid relegation from the top tier. Walters played five league games and four FA Cup matches to help them reach the quarterfinals. He also helped the club remain in the Premier League before being released and joining Swindon Town.

CHAPTER 7:

SENSATIONAL STRIKERS & FORWARDS

QUIZ TIME!

1. Which player made the most appearances in all competitions for the Saints?

   a. Eric Day

   b. Mick Channon

   c. Arthur Dominy

   d. Terry Paine

2. Kevin Keegan was the first Southampton player to win the PFA Players' Player of the Year award.

   a. True

   b. False

3. How many goals did Adam Lallana score in the 2009-10 domestic league season?

   a. 8

   b. 11

   c. 15

   d. 22

4. Which player appeared in all 38 games in the 2014-15 Premier League?

   a. Graziano Pellè
   b. Shane Long
   c. Dušan Tadić
   d. Sadio Mané

5. Shane Long left which club to join the Saints?

   a. AFC Bournemouth
   b. Hull City FC
   c. Stoke City FC
   d. Wolverhampton Wanderers

6. Which player scored eight goals in all competitions in 2018-19?

   a. Mohamed Elyounoussi
   b. Michael Obafemi
   c. Manolo Gabbiadini
   d. Danny Ings

7. Iain Dowie was shown nine yellow cards in the 1992-93 Premier League.

   a. True
   b. False

8. How many appearances did Mick Channon make in all competitions for Southampton?

   a. 584
   b. 607

c. 725

d. 803

9. From which club did Charlie Austin join the Saints?

    a. Leeds United

    b. Newcastle United

    c. West Bromwich Albion

    d. Queens Park Rangers

10. How many goals did Marians Pahars tally in the 2000-01 Premier League?

    a. 15

    b. 13

    c. 9

    d. 5

11. Who scored 13 goals in the 2013-14 domestic league season?

    a. Daniel Osvaldo

    b. Rickie Lambert

    c. Sam Gallagher

    d. Adam Lallana

12. Eric Day played his entire pro career for the Saints.

    a. True

    b. False

13. How many appearances did Terry Paine make in all competitions?

    a. 649

    b. 772

c. 816

d. 835

14. Which player appeared in 41 games in all competitions in 2017-18?

   a. Charlie Austin

   b. Sofiane Boufal

   c. Dušan Tadić

   d. Nathan Redmond

15. How many goals did Gareth Bale score in his only full season with the Saints?

   a. 3

   b. 5

   c. 8

   d. 13

16. Lee Bernard was shown two red cards in the 2010-11 domestic league season.

   a. True

   b. False

17. Which club did Sadio Mané leave to join the Saints?

   a. RB Salzburg FC

   b. RC Strasbourg Alsace

   c. AS Monaco

   d. Bayer 04 Leverkusen

18. How many appearances did Eric Day make in all competitions?

a. 396

b. 422

c. 578

d. 726

19. Who appeared in 42 matches in all competitions in 2003-04?

a. Brett Ormerod

b. Fabrice Fernandes

c. Kevin Phillips

d. James Beattie

20. Gareth Bale recorded 15 assists in the 2006-07 Championship League season.

a. True

b. False

QUIZ ANSWERS

1. D – Terry Paine

2. A – True

3. C – 15

4. A – Graziano Pellè

5. B – Hull City FC

6. D – Danny Ings

7. A – True

8. B – 607

9. D – Queens Park Rangers

10. C – 9

11. B – Rickie Lambert

12. A – True

13. C – 816

14. C – Dušan Tadić

15. B – 5

16. B – False

17. A – RB Salzburg FC

18. B – 422

19. D – James Beattie

20. B – False

DID YOU KNOW?

1. Forwards who have been named Southampton's Player of the Year between 1973-74 and 2019-20 are: 1973-44, Mick Channon; 1979-80, Phil Boyer; 1981-82, Kevin Keegan; 1990-91, Alan Shearer; 1996-97, Egil Østenstad; 1998-99, James Beattie; 2002-03, James Beattie; 2004-05, Peter Crouch; 2009-10, Rickie Lambert; 2011-12, Rickie Lambert; 2015-16, Shane Long; and 2019-20, Danny Ings.

2. Known as one of England's best strikers ever, Alan Shearer kicked off his pro career with the club from 1988 to 1992. He scored a hat-trick in his first start and contributed 43 goals in 158 appearances before joining Blackburn Rovers for what was then a British record transfer fee of £3.6 million. He later joined hometown team Newcastle United for a world-record £15 million. Shearer was Southampton's Player of the Year for 1990-91, led the team in scoring in 1991-92, and went on to win several individual awards later in his career. He tried football management after hanging up his boots and became a popular television pundit. Shearer was inducted into the English Football Hall of Fame and is currently the all-time leader in Premier League scoring with 260 goals in 441 games.

3. Leading the Saints in scoring in 1999-2000 and 2001-02 was fan favorite Marians Pahars. The Latvian international

arrived from Skonto in his homeland and scored both goals in Southampton's 2-0 victory over Everton on the final day of the 1999-2000 season to avoid relegation. He chipped in with 45 goals in 156 appearances before leaving in 2006 to continue his career in Cyprus. The three-time Latvian Footballer of the Year (1999, 2000, 2001) later managed the Latvian national men's team, and as of 2021, he was the boss of Siena in Italy.

4. Edric "Ted" Bates joined in 1937 after playing for Folland Aircraft, his local works team, and went on to score 64 times in 217 appearances before retiring in 1953. He peaked as a player between 1947 and 1951 when he formed an effective partnership with Charlie Wayman. As a manager, Bates took over in 1955 and led the team from the third division to the top-flight in 1966. He handed the reins to Lawrie McMenemy in 1973 but remained as an assistant. Bates then joined the board and became director and president of the club. There's a statue of Bates outside St. Mary's Stadium in his honor. Ted was the son of Eddie Bates and grandson of Billy Bates, two well-known cricket players.

5. After graduating from the Saints' youth system, Steve Moran made his first-team debut in 1979 and remained until joining Leicester City in 1986 for a fee of £300,000. In between, he helped the club finish as First Division runner-up in 1983-84, and he tallied 99 goals in 229 appearances. He was the first Southampton player to win the PFA Young Player of the Year award, in 1981-82.

Moran led the side in scoring three times and netted 25 goals in 1983-84.

6. After arriving from Blackburn Rovers in 1998, English international James Beattie became the Saints' most productive forward of the early 2000s. He led the team in scoring in 2000-01, 2002-03, and 2003-04 and helped the side reach the 2002-03 FA Cup final only to lose 1-0 to Arsenal. Beattie was also named the team's Player of the Year for 1998-99 and 2002-03. After chipping in with 76 goals in 235 outings, he was transferred to Everton for £6 million. After retiring, he turned to coaching.

7. English international Rickie Lambert arrived in 2009 from Bristol Rovers and led the squad in scoring from 2009-10 to 2012-13. He won the second-tier League One Golden Boot in 2009-10 and 2020-11 with 36 and 21 goals, respectively, and was Southampton's Player of the Year for 2009-10 and 2011-12. He helped the team rise from League One to the Premier League by finishing as runner-up in League One in 2010-11 and in the Championship League in 2011-12. Lambert also helped the side win the Football League Trophy in 2009-10 and won several other individual awards with the club while scoring 117 times in 235 games before joining Liverpool in 2014.

8. English international Martin Chivers kicked off his pro career with 108 goals in 190 games with the Saints from 1962 to 1968 before joining Tottenham Hotspur. He made his debut as a 17-year-old and shared the team scoring

lead in 1963-64 with Terry Paine, then led the team and Second Division in scoring in 1965-66 with 30 goals. The team finished as runner-up that season to earn promotion to the top-flight. In January 1968, Chivers moved to Tottenham Hotspur for a reported British transfer record £125,000, with Frank Saul also moving from Spurs to The Dell.

9. Leading the Saints with 30 goals and the First Division with 26 in 1981-82 as well as being named the club's Player of the Year was English international sensation and captain Kevin Keegan. Known as "Mighty Mouse," the 5 foot, 8 inch forward had already won numerous team and individual trophies with Liverpool and Hamburger SV before arriving at The Dell from Germany in 1980. He was also voted the PFA Player of the Year for 1981-82. A few days before the start of the 1982-83 campaign, Keegan signed with Newcastle United for a fee of £100,000. The English Football Hall-of-Famer scored 42 goals in 80 games with Southampton and later managed several top-flight teams as well as England.

10. Center-forward Charles Wayman became a Southampton legend after World War II when he arrived from Newcastle United in 1947. The former miner formed a fantastic partnership with Ted Bates and tallied 77 goals in 107 appearances. He led the team in scoring for three straight seasons and led the Second Division in 1948-49 with 32 goals, including a team-record five in a 6-0 win over Leicester City. He joined Preston North End in 1950

and retired in 1958 due to a knee injury while playing with Darlington. Wayman later coached Evenwood Town before becoming a sales manager for the Scottish and Newcastle brewery. Wayman's brother Frank was also a professional soccer player.

CHAPTER 8:

NOTABLE TRANSFERS & SIGNINGS

QUIZ TIME!

1. Who has been Southampton's most expensive transfer signing as of April 2021?

    a. Sadio Mané

    b. Danny Ings

    c. Jannik Vestergaard

    d. Guido Carillo

2. Southampton sold Morgan Schneiderlin to Manchester United for a fee of £23 million.

    a. True

    b. False

3. Who was the club's most expensive transfer signing in 2002-03?

    a. Antti Niemi

    b. David Prutton

    c. Michael Svensson

    d. Danny Higginbotham

4. Which player commanded the club's highest transfer fee when he was sold?

    a. Virgil van Dijk
    b. Sadio Mané
    c. Luke Shaw
    d. Adam Lallana

5. The Saints signed Danny Osvaldo from which club?

    a. Club Brugge KV
    b. Valencia CF
    c. AS Roma
    d. OGC Nice

6. Who was the club's most expensive transfer signing in 2009-10?

    a. Morgan Schneiderlin
    b. Richard Chaplow
    c. Rickie Lambert
    d. José Fonte

7. The Saints transferred Alex Oxlade-Chamberlain to Aston Villa for a fee of £14 million in 2011-12.

    a. True
    b. False

8. How much did Southampton pay to acquire Sadio Mané?

    a. £32 million
    b. £24 million
    c. £20.70 million
    d. £17 million

9. Which club did the Saints sign Danny Ings from?

    a. Hull City FC

    b. Dorchester Town FC

    c. Liverpool FC

    d. Chelsea FC

10. What was the transfer fee Southampton received for Luke Shaw?

    a. £46 million

    b. £33.75 million

    c. £29 million

    d. £22 million

11. Who was the Saints' most expensive transfer signing in 2016-17?

    a. Sofiane Boufal

    b. Manolo Gabbiadini

    c. Pierre-Emile Højbjerg

    d. Nathan Redmond

12. Southampton acquired Marians Pahars for a fee of £2.08 million in 1998-99.

    a. True

    b. False

13. Which side was defender Luke Shaw transferred to?

    a. Manchester United

    b. Arsenal FC

    c. Olympique Lyon

    d. Inter Milan

14. What was the transfer fee the Saints received for Virgil van Dijk?

    a. £48.70 million
    b. £51 million
    c. £66 million
    d. £76.19 million

15. Who was the Saints' most expensive departure in 2004-05?

    a. Peter Crouch
    b. Wayne Bridge
    c. James Beattie
    d. Theo Walcott

16. Southampton signed Jannik Vestergaard from German team Bayern Munich.

    a. True
    b. False

17. Which player did Southampton acquire from Juventus in 2017-18?

    a. Mario Lemina
    b. Wesley Hoedt
    c. Mohamed Elyounoussi
    d. Moussa Djenepo

18. How much did the Saints pay to acquire Danny Ings from Liverpool?

    a. £31 million
    b. £25.60 million

c. £23 million

d. £19.98 million

19. Which side did Southampton sign goalkeeper Fraser Forster from?

a. Celtic FC

b. Fulham FC

c. Aberdeen FC

d. Stoke City FC

20. Southampton did not make an official transfer signing in 2012-13.

a. True

b. False

QUIZ ANSWERS

1. C – Jannik Vestergaard

2. B – False

3. B – David Prutton

4. A – Virgil van Dijk

5. C – AS Roma

6. D – José Fonte

7. B – False

8. C – £20.70 million

9. C – Liverpool FC

10. B – £33.75 million

11. A – Sofiane Boufal

12. B – False

13. A – Manchester United

14. D – £76.19 million

15. C – James Beattie

16. B – False

17. A – Mario Lemina

18. D – £19.98 million

19. A – Celtic FC

20. B – False

DID YOU KNOW?

1. The five highest transfer fees paid by Southampton as of April 2021 are: defender Jannik Vestergaard from Borussia Mönchengladbach for £22.5 million in 2018-19; winger Sadio Mané from Red Bull Salzburg for £20.7 million in 2014-15; forward Danny Ings from Liverpool FC for £19.98 million in 2019-20; forward Guido Carrillo from AS Monaco for £19.8 million in 2017-18; and winger Sofiane Boufal from LOSC Lille for £16.83 million in 2016-17.

2. The five highest transfer fees received by the Saints as of April 2021 are: defender Virgil van Dijk to Liverpool FC for £76.19 million in 2017-18; winger Sadio Mané to Liverpool FC for £37.08 million in 2016-17; defender Luke Shaw to Manchester United for £33.75 million in 2014-15; midfielder Morgan Schneiderlin to Manchester United for £31.5 million in 2015-16; and midfielder Adam Lallana to Liverpool FC for £27.9 million in 2014-15.

3. Forward David "Danny" Wallace made his Saints debut at the age of 16 years and 313 days in 1980 to become the team's youngest first-team player at the time. He became a regular in 1982-83 when he tallied 12 goals in 35 appearances and played 14 times for the England under-21 side. A fan favorite due to his speed and scoring talent, he helped the team finish as First Division runner-up in

1983-84. Wallace scored 79 goals in 317 games, and in 1988, his brothers Rodney and Raymond joined the club. It was the first time three brothers played for the same English top-flight side since 1920. In September 1989, Danny was sold for a reported £1.2 million to Manchester United to set a new transfer record for a Saints player. His career came to an end in 1996 when he was diagnosed with multiple sclerosis.

4. Manchester United bought English international defender Luke Shaw from the Saints in July 2014 for £33.75 million just days before he turned 19 years old. This made him one of the most expensive teenage transfers in soccer history. The left-back joined the Southampton academy at the age of eight and made his first-team debut as a 16-year-old. He played 67 games before being sold and was one of six players shortlisted for the PFA Young Player of the Year award in 2013-14. He was named to that season's PFA Premier League Team of the Year. Shaw was still with Man United in 2020-21 and was named the team's Players' Player of the Year and Player of the Year for 2018-19.

5. English international midfielder Alex Oxlade-Chamberlain was another high-priced teenager as he was sold by the Saints to Arsenal for £12.42 million in 2011 at the age of 17. He went on to play for the under-18, -19, and -21 levels for England and has appeared in 35 games for the senior side. He spent his youth career at Southampton and played twice in the senior side in 2009-10 and 41 times in 2010-11, scoring

10 goals. Oxlade-Chamberlain was named to the PFA League One Team of the Year for 2010-11. His career has been plagued with injuries, and he was sold to Liverpool by Arsenal for £34.2 million in 2017. He's still with Liverpool and had notched 43 goals in 340 career club games as of April 5, 2021.

6. Arsenal shelled out £18.21 million to Southampton for 19-year-old defender Calum Chambers in the summer of 2014. He joined the Saints at the age of seven and was promoted to the first-team in 2012-13. He made his debut in August 2012 and, a year later, signed a new four-year deal with the team. Chambers played 25 games with the club before moving to Arsenal. He's played for England at the under-17, -19, and -21 levels and three times for the senior side. Chambers can play right-back and center-back, and after being sent on loan with Middlesbrough and Fulham, he was back with Arsenal in 2020-21. He was named Fulham's Player of the Year for 2018-19.

7. The legend of Aly Dia and his 53 minutes of top-flight action for Southampton in 1996 has never gone away. The native of Senegal played in France, Finland, and Germany early in his career before ending up in England with Blyth Spartans. Rumor has it that Dia's friend contacted the Saints, claiming to be Liberian international star George Weah, and recommended him to the club, saying Dia was his cousin. Dia headed to Southampton to train with the team and was brought on as a sub against Leeds. However, he seemed to be lost on the pitch and was substituted

himself after 53 minutes. Dia reportedly signed a month-long contract with the club but was released after 14 days.

8. Danish international defender Jannik Vestergaard played youth soccer in his homeland before starting his pro career in Germany with TSG 1899 Hoffenheim in 2010-11. He was transferred to Werder Bremen in January 2015 for £4.05 million and moved to Borussia Mönchengladbach in June 2016 for £11.25 million. Vestergaard then became Southampton's most expensive signing ever on July 13, 2018, when he was acquired for £22.5 million. He signed a four-year contract and since then has appeared in 70 matches with the Saints as of April 2021 and has scored four goals.

9. The biggest transfer fee the club received was £76.19 million from Liverpool for Dutch international defender Virgil van Dijk. He began his pro career with Groningen in 2011 before being sold to Glasgow Celtic in 2013 for £2.48 million. He helped the team win two league titles and the Scottish League Cup and was named to the PFA Scotland Premier League Team of the Year for 2013-14 and 2014-15 and was the Celtic's Players' Player of the Year for 2013-14. The Saints paid £14.13 million for van Dijk in September 2015, and he was the club's Player of the Season for 2015-16. He chipped in with seven goals in 80 games before Liverpool bought him in January 2018. Since then, he's won several team and individual titles with the club, including the Premier League and European Champions League.

10. Southampton has made several other big-money deals with Liverpool. Winger Sadio Mané was sold to the Merseyside club for £37.08 million in July 2016 after the Saints acquired him from Red Bull Salzburg for £20.7 million in September 2014. Mané led the team in scoring in 2015-16 and notched 25 goals in 75 games before being sold. The Saints also sold English international midfielder and the team's 2013-14 Player of the Year Adam Lallana to Liverpool for £27.9 million in July 2014 after 60 goals and 265 appearances with the club. In addition, forward Danny Ings was bought from Liverpool for £19.98 million in July 2019. He then led the club in scoring in 2019-20 with 25 goals and was named the club's Player of the Year.

CHAPTER 9:

ODDS & ENDS

QUIZ TIME!

1. What is the most wins the Saints have recorded in a Premier League season as of 2020?

    a. 12
    b. 15
    c. 18
    d. 22

2. Southampton's longest winning streak in the domestic league as of 2020 is 10 in 2011.

    a. True
    b. False

3. The first time the club won a Southern League match, 11-0 on December 28, 1901, was against which team?

    a. Queens Park Rangers
    b. Kettering Town FC
    c. Brentford FC
    d. Northampton Town FC

4. Who was the oldest player to make an appearance for the Saints at 39 years and 18 days old?

    a. Peter Shilton

    b. Bruce Grobbelaar

    c. Dennis Wise

    d. Kelvin Davis

5. What is the most wins Southampton has recorded in a single domestic league season at any level as of 2019-20?

    a. 33

    b. 28

    c. 26

    d. 23

6. Southampton's biggest Premier League defeat at home was a 9-0 to which outfit?

    a. Burnley FC

    b. Tottenham Hotspur

    c. Leicester City FC

    d. Manchester City FC

7. As of 2020, the Saints have spent 50 seasons in the top-flight of English football.

    a. True

    b. False

8. How many games did the squad lose in the 1993-94 Premier League?

    a. 11

    b. 18

c. 23

d. 27

9. Who scored the fastest hat-trick in Premier League history as of 2019-20 in two minutes and 56 seconds?

    a. Rickie Lambert

    b. Marians Pahars

    c. Matt Le Tissier

    d. Sadio Mané

10. What is the most goals scored by the Saints in a domestic league season as of 2019-20?

    a. 77

    b. 85

    c. 99

    d. 112

11. On October 18, 2014, which player tied the Premier League record for most assists in a game with four?

    a. Dušan Tadić

    b. Victor Wanyama

    c. Graziano Pellè

    d. Jack Cork

12. The Southampton FC Women club was founded in 1982.

    a. True

    b. False

13. The Saints' biggest victory in the Premier League was an 8-0 win against what club?

a. Oldham Athletic

b. Watford FC

c. Sunderland AFC

d. Crystal Palace FC

14. Who has been Southampton's youngest first-team player at the age of 16 years and 142 days?

a. Luke Shaw

b. Alex Oxlade-Chamberlain

c. Theo Wolcott

d. Gareth Bale

15. The South Coast Derby is the nickname for the rivalry between Southampton and which other club?

a. Bournemouth FC

b. Reading FC

c. Brighton & Hove Albion

d. Portsmouth FC

16. The Saints went on a 19-game unbeaten streak between September 5 and December 31, 1921.

a. True

b. False

17. Which player scored a Premier League goal 7.69 seconds into a match against Watford FC?

a. Shane Long

b. Pierre-Emile Højbjerg

c. Bradley Wright-Phillips

d. Steven Davis

18. How many seasons has Southampton spent in the fourth tier of the English football system?

    a. 0
    b. 1
    c. 3
    d. 5

19. Who was the first player to score a goal at The Dell for the Saints?

    a. Harry Wood
    b. Walter Keay
    c. Thomas Nicol
    d. James McKenzie

20. Southampton's highest home stadium attendance as of 2020 was 32,533 in a match against Portsmouth FC.

    a. True
    b. False

QUIZ ANSWERS

1. C – 18

2. A – True

3. D – Northampton Town FC

4. D – Kelvin Davis

5. B – 28

6. C – Leicester City FC

7. B – False

8. C – 23

9. D – Sadio Mané

10. D – 112

11. A – Dušan Tadić

12. B – False

13. C – Sunderland AFC

14. C – Theo Wolcott

15. D – Portsmouth FC

16. A – True

17. A – Shane Long

18. A – 0

19. B – Walter Keay

20. B – False

DID YOU KNOW?

1. Since 1898, the Saints' permanent home ground was known as The Dell, which had a capacity of approximately 30,000. The club then moved to St. Mary's Stadium in August 2001 with its capacity of 32,384. The venue's record attendance is 32,363, which was set on April 28, 2012, when the Saints took on Coventry City in a Championship League game.

2. Parts of The Dell had to be rebuilt in 1941 because stored munitions exploded, and the team played some home games at Dew Lane, Eastleigh, until October 1941. In 1950, it became the first soccer stadium in England to boast permanent floodlights. When The Dell was converted to an all-seat stadium in 1993, its capacity was reduced to approximately 15,000, making it the smallest top-flight ground in England.

3. Southampton has had a long-standing rivalry with Portsmouth FC due to the geographical closeness of the two cities and clubs. The fixture between the two teams is known as the South Coast Derby. The club was also briefly forced to play some home matches at Portsmouth's Fratton Park ground during World War II when a bomb landed on the pitch at The Dell. It left an 18-foot crater and damaged an underground culvert, causing the pitch to flood.

4. The team's anthem is the popular hymn and jazz song "When the Saints Go Marching In." The original club crest was the same as the city of Southampton's crest until the 1970s, when a contest was held to design a new one. The winning design was used for approximately 20 years until it was slightly modified.

5. Southampton operates a successful youth academy and B team with several squads for players from the age of eight to 23. The academy has produced several international players in the past, such as Adam Lallana, Alex Oxlade-Chamberlain, James Ward-Prowse, Calum Chambers, Luke Shaw, Alan Shearer, and Theo Walcott of England, as well as Gareth Bale of Wales and Michael Obafemi of the Republic of Ireland.

6. The Saints first earned promotion to the top-flight First Division in 1966. Since then, and as of 2020-21, the team has played just 11 seasons outside of the top-flight in two separate stints. The longest spell was between 2005 and 2013 when the Saints played in the second-tier Championship League and third-tier League One.

7. Rupert Lowe resigned as the club's chairman in June 2006, and major shareholder Michael Wilde took over the position. He then stepped down in February 2007 when the board sought new investment, and Leon Crouch took over as acting chairman. All of the board members except one resigned in July 2008 as Wilde and Rupert Lowe took over. However, the club had to sell and loan out players

to keep afloat financially. In addition, sections of St. Mary's Stadium were closed off to help cut costs.

8. In April 2009, the soccer club's parent company was placed into administration, and the team was soon hit with a 10-point penalty in the season's standings. However, Southampton was being relegated to the third-tier League One anyway after finishing second to last in the Championship League. Therefore, the 10 points were deducted from the team at the beginning of the 2009-10 campaign. The club was unable to pay staff wages at this time and asked its employees to work unpaid until things were sorted out.

9. The club faced imminent bankruptcy without a new buyer, and the day was saved when Markus Liebherr purchased Southampton FC in the summer of 2009. Liebherr passed away a year later, and his daughter Katharina then took over as the owner. Chinese businessman Gao Jisheng purchased a controlling interest in Southampton FC from Katharina Liebherr in August 2017.

10. Southampton FC Women is an English women's soccer club currently competing in the FA Women's National League Division One South West, which is the fourth tier of the nation's women's league system. The club originated in 1970 as Southampton Women's FC when it was formed by female fans of the men's side and became associated with the men's club in 2018. Also nicknamed the Saints, the team plays its home games at Testwood Park in Totton, which has a capacity of 3,000.

CHAPTER 10:

DOMESTIC COMPETITION

QUIZ TIME!

1. How many League Cups have the Saints won as of 2020?

   a. 0

   b. 1

   c. 3

   d. 6

2. Southampton has never won a top-flight First Division/ Premier League title.

   a. True

   b. False

3. Which season did the team reach the FA Cup final for the first time?

   a. 1896-97

   b. 1899-1900

   c. 1948-49

   d. 1975-76

4. How many times did Southampton win the Southern League championship?

    a. 3
    b. 5
    c. 6
    d. 9

5. Which club did the Saints face in the 1978-79 Football League Cup final?

    a. Derby County FC
    b. Brighton & Hove Albion
    c. Nottingham Forest FC
    d. Leeds United

6. Which season did Southampton win the Third Division title?

    a. 1920-21
    b. 1926-27
    c. 1947-48
    d. 1959-60

7. The Saints were two-time winners of the Western League.

    a. True
    b. False

8. Southampton won its first FA Cup final against what club?

    a. Manchester United
    b. Blackpool FC

c. Leicester City FC

d. Crystal Palace FC

9. How many times did the Saints win the Hampshire Senior Cup?

    a. 7

    b. 5

    c. 3

    d. 1

10. Who scored the game-winning goal in the 2009-10 Football League Trophy final?

    a. Papa Waigo

    b. Michail Antonio

    c. Rickie Lambert

    d. Adam Lallana

11. Which was the first side the Saints faced in an FA Cup final?

    a. Millwall Athletic

    b. Sheffield United

    c. Tottenham Hotspur

    d. Bury FC

12. Southampton shared the 1975-76 FA Charity Shield honors with Liverpool FC.

    a. True

    b. False

13. How many points did Southampton post to win their first Southern League title?

a. 35

b. 31

c. 27

d. 24

14. The Saints faced which club in the 2002-03 FA Cup final?

    a. Tottenham Hotspur

    b. Wolverhampton Wanderers

    c. Arsenal FC

    d. Oxford United

15. Which season did Southampton finish as First Division runner-up?

    a. 1968-69

    b. 1976-77

    c. 1983-84

    d. 1989-90

16. The Saints were runners-up to Chelsea in the 1991-92 Full Members' Cup final.

    a. True

    b. False

17. Who netted the game-winning goal in the 1975-76 FA Cup final?

    a. Paul Gilchrist

    b. Peter Osgood

    c. Nick Holmes

    d. Bobby Stokes

18. How many points did the Saints earn in the 1959-60 Third Division?

    a. 61
    b. 57
    c. 73
    d. 64

19. How many times have the Saints been runners-up in the League Cup as of 2020?

    a. 5
    b. 4
    c. 2
    d. 1

20. Rickie Lambert won the Man of the Match in the 2009-10 Football League Trophy final.

    a. True
    b. False

QUIZ ANSWERS

1. A – 0

2. A – True

3. B – 1899-1900

4. C – 6

5. C – Nottingham Forest FC

6. D – 1959-60

7. B – False

8. A – Manchester United

9. C – 3

10. D – Adam Lallana

11. D – Bury FC

12. B – False

13. A – 35

14. C – Arsenal FC

15. C – 1983-84

16. B – False

17. D – Bobby Stokes

18. A – 61

19. C – 2

20. A – True

DID YOU KNOW?

1. Southampton has yet to win a top-tier or second-tier championship in England. They have won a pair of third-tier league titles, though, along with an English FA Cup. The Saints have also yet to hoist an English League Cup and FA Charity/Community Shield, but they have won several minor English trophies.

2. The closest the Saints have come to capturing a top-flight crown as of 2020-21 was by finishing as runners-up to Liverpool in the First Division by three points in 1983-84. They finished as runners-up in the second-tier Second Division/Championship League in 1965-66, 1977-78, and 2011-12.

3. Southampton topped the table in 1921-22 in the Third Division South and again in 1959-60 in the Third Division. They were also runners-up in the Third Division in 1920-21 and in the third-tier League One in 2010-11.

4. Before joining the English Football League in 1920, the Saints competed in the Southern League and Western League. They were crowned champions of the Southern League in 1896-97, 1897-98, 1898-99, 1900-01, 1902-03, and 1903-04. They finished as runners-up in the Western League in 1903-04, 1905-06, and 1907-08 and were also Section A winners in 1907-08.

5. The club's lone FA Cup victory was celebrated in 1975-76, and they finished as runners-up in 1899-1900, 1901-02, and 2002-03. The Saints have never won a League Cup but finished as runners-up in both 1978-79 and 2016-17.

6. The Saints' FA Cup victory came on May 1, 1976, in front of more than 99,000 fans at Wembley Stadium. They took on Manchester United, which had finished in third place in the First Division that season while underdog Southampton finished the campaign in sixth place in the Second Division. The favorites were beaten 1-0, thanks to a goal from Bobby Stokes in the 83rd minute. It was the club's first major trophy and the last time Queen Elizabeth presented the silverware to the winners.

7. Southampton's first FA Cup final appearance ended in a 4-0 defeat to Bury FC in 1899-1900 on April 21, 1900. They next reached the final in 1901-02 and played to a 1-1 draw with Sheffield United on April 19, 1902. A replay was needed a week later, and they won 2-1. They last reached the FA Cup final in 2002-03 on May 17, 2003, and were downed 1-0 by Arsenal.

8. The first time the club reached the League Cup final was in 1978-79 when they faced Nottingham Forest with over 96,000 fans in attendance. Forest was favored as reigning First Division champions and League Cup holders. Southampton took the lead after 16 minutes, but Forest stormed back with three second-half goals, in the 51st, 79th, and 83rd minutes. The Saints then made it interesting with a goal two minutes from time but lost 3-2.

9. Southampton's only other League Cup final came in 2016-17 in front of 85,000 supporters. Once again, they were the underdogs and were edged 3-2, this time by Manchester United. Man United led 2-0 thanks to goals in the 19th and 38th minutes. The Saints' Manolo Gabbiadini then scored just before and after halftime to level things at 2-2. They then conceded in the 87th minute, though, when Zlatan Ibrahimović notched his second goal of the game to win the cup for United.

10. The Saints won the minor Football League Trophy (EFL Trophy) in 2009-10 by beating Carlisle United 4-1 at Wembley Stadium with over 73,000 fans on hand. This is an annual English association football knockout competition open to the 48 clubs from the third and fourth tiers of the league as well as 16 under-21 squads from the Premier League and second-tier Championship League.

CHAPTER 11:

EUROPE & BEYOND

QUIZ TIME!

1. Which club did Southampton play in its first European match?

    a. Third Lanark Athletic Club

    b. RC Lens

    c. Motherwell FC

    d. FC Bordeaux

2. The first international competition Southampton participated in was the 1961-62 Anglo-Franco Friendship Cup.

    a. True

    b. False

3. What was the first major international tournament the Saints played in?

    a. Inter-Cities Fairs Cup

    b. European Cup Winners' Cup

    c. UEFA Cup

    d. UEFA Champions League

4. How many times have the Saints participated in the UEFA Cup/Europa League as of 2020?

   a. 3
   b. 5
   c. 7
   d. 10

5. What was the outcome of Southampton's first international game?

   a. 1-0 win
   b. 1-1 draw
   c. 2-1 win
   d. 3-0 loss

6. Which club eliminated the Saints in the 1969-70 Inter-Cities Fairs Cup?

   a. FC Twente
   b. Rosenborg BK
   c. Vitória de Guimarães
   d. Newcastle United

7. Southampton were joint winners of the 1961-62 Anglo-Franco Friendship Cup.

   a. True
   b. False

8. Which year did the club participate in the Anglo-Italian League Cup?

   a. 1982
   b. 1976

c. 1971

d. 1969

9. Southampton played which side in the 2015-16 UEFA Europa League playoff round?

a. Athletic Bilbao

b. FC Midtjylland

c. Borussia Dortmund

d. PAOK FC

10. What round did the Saints reach in the 1976-77 European Cup Winners' Cup?

a. Finals

b. Semifinals

c. Quarterfinals

d. Second round

11. Which season did Southampton reach the final round of the Texaco Cup?

a. 1966-67

b. 1969-70

c. 1972-73

d. 1974-75

12. The Saints have qualified for the UEFA Champions League twice as of 2020.

a. True

b. False

13. Southampton played what outfit in the 1976 Anglo-Italian League Cup?

a. S.S.C. Napoli

b. West Ham United

c. Torino FC

d. Swindon Town FC

14. Who scored Southampton's only goal in the two legs of the 1974-75 Texaco Cup final?

   a. Mick Channon

   b. Michael Gilchrist

   c. Bobby Stokes

   d. Pat Earles

15. Which round of the 2016-17 UEFA Europa League did the Saints reach?

   a. Quarterfinals

   b. Second round

   c. First round

   d. Group stage

16. Southampton has qualified for the Inter-Cities Fairs Cup just once.

   a. True

   b. False

17. Which team did the Saints NOT play on their way to the 1974-75 Texaco Cup final?

   a. Luton Town FC

   b. Ranger FC

   c. Oldham Athletic

   d. Birmingham City FC

18. How many European Cup/Champions League tournaments has Southampton participated in as of 2020?

    a. 3
    b. 6
    c. 0
    d. 9

19. Southampton faced what squad in the 1976-77 European Cup Winners' Cup quarterfinals?

    a. PFC Levski Sofia
    b. Hamburger SV
    c. R.S.C. Anderlecht
    d. Atlético Madrid

20. Middlesbrough FC eliminated the Saints in the 1974-75 Texaco Cup final.

    a. True
    b. False

QUIZ ANSWERS

1. D – FC Bordeaux

2. B – False

3. A – Inter-Cities Fairs Cup

4. C – 7

5. C – 2-1 win

6. D – Newcastle United

7. A – True

8. B – 1976

9. B – FC Midtjylland

10. C – Quarterfinals

11. D – 1974-75

12. B – False

13. A – S.S.C. Napoli

14. A – Mick Channon

15. D – Group stage

16. A – True

17. D – Birmingham City FC

18. C – 0

19. C – R.S.C. Anderlecht

20. B – False

DID YOU KNOW?

1. Southampton first qualified for a major European competition in 1969-70. Overall, the club has participated in the Inter-Cities Fairs Cup, the European Cup Winners' Cup, the UEFA Europa League, the Anglo-French Friendship Cup, the Anglo-Italian League Cup, and the Texaco Cup.

2. The club's very first venture into Europe came in 1961-62 when it entered a minor tournament known as the Anglo-French Friendship Cup. This was a short-lived inter-league event that lasted just two seasons. It consisted of four English teams competing against four French clubs. There was no individual winner as the nation whose teams won the most games was declared the champion. In 1961-62, Southampton beat Bordeaux 2-1 at home but lost 2-0 in France, and the English League won by posting two wins, a loss, and a draw.

3. The first major European tournament the Saints played in was the 1969-70 Inter-Cities Fairs Cup. The Saints' first opponent was Rosenborg of Norway. Southampton was edged 1-0 away but won 2-0 at home in the second leg. They then faced Portuguese side Vitória de Guimarães and drew 3-3 away before winning 5-1 at home. In the round of 16, the Saints drew 0-0 away and 1-1 at home with Newcastle United, which saw them eliminated due to the away-goals rule.

4. After the Saints finished in seventh place in the league in 1970-71, they qualified for the 1971-72 UEFA Cup. They faced a Spanish team, Athletic Bilbao, in the first round and came from behind to win the first leg 2-1 at The Dell. However, two weeks later, they were beaten 2-0 away after conceding a late goal and were downed 3-2 on aggregate.

5. Southampton qualified for the 1974-75 minor tournament known as the Texaco Cup. The teams were placed in four groups with the top two sides from each group advancing to play a knockout stage with four teams from Scotland. The Saints drew Luton Town 1-1 away, beat Leyton Orient 2-1 at home, and beat West Ham United 2-0 at home to top their group. They faced Glasgow Rangers in the knockout stage and won 3-1 away in the first leg and 2-0 home in the second leg. They then beat Oldham Athletic 3-1 away and 2-1 at home. In the Texaco Cup final against Newcastle United, Southampton won the first leg 1-0 at home and lost the second leg 1-0 away, meaning it needed to be decided in extra time. Newcastle scored twice in the extra stanza to win 3-1 on aggregate.

6. Second Division Southampton upset Manchester United 1-0 in the 1975-76 FA Cup final and qualified for the 1976-77 European Cup Winners' Cup. The Saints faced Olympique Marseille in the first round and won the first leg 4-0 at home while losing the second leg 2-1 away to advance 5-2 on aggregate. They then met Irish Cup winners Carrick Rangers and won 9-3 on aggregate thanks to a 5-2 away win in Northern Ireland in the first leg and a 4-1 victory at

home. They faced Belgian Cup champions R.S.C. Anderlecht in the quarterfinals, where they dropped the first leg 2-0 away and won 2-1 at home to lose 3-2 on aggregate.

7. The Saints qualified for the UEFA Cup two straight times in 1981-82 and 1982-83. In 1981-82, they traveled to Ireland to play Limerick FC and won 3-0 away while drawing 1-1 at home. They met Sporting Clube de Portugal in the second round and were eliminated due to a 4-2 loss at home and a 0-0 away draw. In 1982-83, they played Swedish team IFK Norrköping and were eliminated on the away-goals rule after drawing 2-2 at The Dell and 0-0 in Sweden.

8. Southampton was right back in the UEFA Cup again in 1984-85 after finishing as runner-up to Liverpool in the First Division in 1983-84. They faced Hamburger SV of Germany in the tournament and drew 0-0 at home in the first leg and were beaten 2-0 away. Almost two decades passed before the Saints played in Europe again, when they competed in the 2003-04 UEFA Cup after finishing as runners-up in the 2002-03 FA Cup by losing 1-0 to Arsenal. They faced Steaua București and were knocked out after drawing 1-0 at home and falling 1-0 away.

9. The Saints entered the Europa League for the first time in 2015-16 after finishing seventh in the league table the previous season. They faced Dutch squad Vitesse Arnhem in the third qualifying round and won 3-0 at home at St.

Mary's Stadium in the first leg and 2-0 away in the second leg. In the qualifying playoff round, the Saints played FC Midtjylland of Denmark and drew 1-1 at home in the first leg only to lose the second leg away 1-0.

10. In 2016-17, the club entered the Europa League group stage after finishing in sixth place in the previous Premier League season. They competed in Group K alongside Inter Milan of Italy, Sparta Prague of the Czech Republic, and Hapoel Be'er Sheva of Israel. The Saints were eliminated from the competition, finishing the group stage with two wins, two draws, and two losses for eight points, with six goals scored and four allowed. Hapoel Be'er Sheva also finished with eight points with the same record and six goals scored and six goals allowed. However, they advanced to the next stage as they drew 0-0 at home with Southampton but drew 1-1 away to win the head-to-head series on the away-goals rule.

CHAPTER 12:

TOP SCORERS

QUIZ TIME!

1. Who is Southampton's all-time leading scorer as of 2020?

   a. Terry Paine

   b. Bill Rawlings

   c. Matt Le Tissier

   d. Mick Channon

2. Southampton has had seven different players win a top-tier Golden Boot award as of 2020.

   a. True

   b. False

3. Who led the Saints in scoring in their first Football League season?

   a. Martin Dunne

   b. Arthur Dominy

   c. Bill Rawlings

   d. Percy Prince

4. Which player holds the club record with seven goals scored in one match?

   a. Fred Harrison
   b. Eric Day
   c. Albert Brown
   d. Rickie Lambert

5. How many goals did Charlie Austin lead the squad with in the 2017-18 Premier League?

   a. 5
   b. 7
   c. 10
   d. 14

6. Which player led the Saints with 12 goals in the 2004-05 domestic league?

   a. Marians Pahars
   b. Henri Camara
   c. Kevin Phillips
   d. Peter Crouch

7. Ron Davies won two First Division Golden Boot awards with Southampton.

   a. True
   b. False

8. How many goals did Terry Paine score in all competitions?

   a. 244
   b. 203

c. 187

d. 175

9. Who led the Saints with 15 goals in their first Premier League season?

   a. Matt Le Tissier

   b. Iain Dowie

   c. Nicky Banger

   d. Neil Maddison

10. What player won a 1981-82 Golden Boot award?

   a. Phil Boyer

   b. Danny Wallace

   c. Steve Moran

   d. Kevin Keegan

11. How many goals did Ron Davies score to win his first Golden Boot award?

   a. 42

   b. 37

   c. 33

   d. 29

12. Charlie Wayman won the 1948-49 Second Division Golden Boot award with 32 goals.

   a. True

   b. False

13. How many goals did Matt Le Tissier score in all competitions for Southampton?

a. 163

b. 182

c. 209

d. 226

14. Who led the side with 22 goals in the 2019-20 Premier League?

    a. Sofiane Boufal

    b. James Ward-Prowse

    c. Danny Ings

    d. Shane Long

15. How many goals did Ricky Lambert score in the 2009-10 domestic league to lead the Saints?

    a. 29

    b. 26

    c. 21

    d. 19

16. Phil Boyer was the first Southampton player to win a Golden Boot in the First Division.

    a. True

    b. False

17. Which two players led Southampton with 11 goals each in the 2015-16 domestic league?

    a. Shane Long and Graziano Pellè

    b. Dušan Tadić and Sadio Mané

    c. Graziano Pellè and Sadio Mané

    d. Shane Long and Dušan Tadić

18. How many goals did Bill Rawlings score in all competitions with the Saints?

   a. 218
   b. 198
   c. 173
   d. 164

19. Who scored 23 goals to win a 2002-03 Golden Boot award?

   a. Paul Telfer
   b. Claus Lundekvam
   c. Dean Richards
   d. James Beattie

20. Three players each scored six goals to lead the club in its first Southern League campaign.

   a. True
   b. False

QUIZ ANSWERS

1. D – Mick Channon

2. B – False

3. C – Bill Rawlings

4. C – Albert Brown

5. B – 7

6. D – Peter Crouch

7. A – True

8. C – 187

9. A – Matt Le Tissier

10. D – Kevin Keegan

11. B – 37

12. A – True

13. C – 209

14. C – Danny Ings

15. A – 29

16. B – False

17. C – Graziano Pellè and Sadio Mané

18. B – 198

19. D – James Beattie

20. A – True

DID YOU KNOW?

1. Welsh international center-forward Ron Davies arrived at The Dell in 1966 from Norwich City for what was then a Saints' transfer record of £55,000 and posted 153 goals in 281 appearances. He topped the First Division in scoring in 1966-67 with 37 goals and tallied 43 in all competitions. He added 28 goals the next season to share the league lead with George Best. Davies also led the team in 1970-71 with 21 goals and joined Portsmouth in April 1973. He later played with Manchester United and finished his career in America from 1976 to 1979. Davies's brother Paul later played for Charlton Athletic.

2. After joining hometown team Southampton from Woolston FC in 1913, Arthur Dominy went on to notch 155 goals in 392 appearances before joining Everton on a free transfer in 1926. He netted 50 goals in 1911-12 for Bitterne Guild and was transferred to the Saints for just £15. Dominy led the side in scoring in four seasons and tallied a career-best 30 in 1914-15 to lead the Southern League. He was with Southampton when the team was admitted to the Football League and helped them win the Third Division South title in 1921-22. Dominy later became a scout for the club and also managed it between 1943 and 1946.

3. Forward Fred "Buzzy" Harrison made his debut for the Saints in 1900-01 when the club won the Southern League championship. The winger eventually moved to center-forward and scored five goals in a game against Wellingborough Town in March 1903. He led or shared the team lead in scoring in four seasons; his best campaign was 1903-04, with 27 goals in 32 league outings as the side once again won the Southern League. Harrison joined Fulham in early 1908 after scoring 156 times in 249 matches for the Saints.

4. Winger Eric Day appeared in 422 matches with the club and chipped in with 158 goals. He played his entire pro career with Southampton from 1945 to 1957 after playing rugby during World War II as an RAF commando. However, after breaking a hand, Day decided to try his luck at soccer. He joined the club just before the Football League resumed following the war and made his official debut in 1946 at the age of 25. Day finished his career by playing non-league football in Kent.

5. In the 1959-60 season, center-forward Derek Reeves tallied a club-record 44 goals in all competitions and that mark is unlikely to be broken in the near future. He also scored 39 league goals that campaign to set a club and Third Division record. Yes, the team was in the third tier at the time, but Reeves notched 173 goals in 311 games with the Saints from 1954 to 1962 and led them in scoring from 1956-57 to 1959-60. Reeves was the cousin of former Norwich City and Manchester City striker Kevin Reeves. He left

Southampton for his hometown club of Bournemouth AFC in 1965.

6. George O'Brien of Scotland joined the club from Leeds United in 1959 after scoring just six goals in 44 league games with the team. He found his scoring touch at The Dell, though, with 180 goals in 291 appearances, and he led the side in scoring four times. He left Southampton in March 1966 for Leyton Orient before moving on in December 1966 to Aldershot, where he finished his playing career. O'Brien ran several pubs and drove a taxi after hanging up his boots, and his son Colin later played with Hereford United.

7. Winger Terry Paine played the most career games with the Saints at 816, and he ranks fourth on the all-time scoring list with 187 goals. The Southampton youth graduate played with the team from 1957 to 1974, making his debut as a 17-year-old, and then joined Hereford United. The English international was also on the 1966 England squad that won the World Cup and helped the Saints win the 1959-60 Third Division title and earn promotion to the top-flight in 1965-66. Paine was named Honorary President of Southampton in January 2013 and later worked as a pundit on South African television.

8. Center-forward Bill Rawlings kicked off his pro career with Southampton from 1918 to 1928. He started when the team was in the Southern League and, from 1920 onward, played in the Football League. He led the team in

scoring seven times from 1920-21 to 1927-28 and helped the side capture the Third Division South title in 1921-22. Rawlings posted 198 goals in 377 matches before joining Manchester United in March 1928, and he hung up his boots in 1933 while playing semi-pro with Newport on the Isle of Wight.

9. With 209 goals in 540 appearances, Matt Le Tissier is ranked second on the club's scoring list. The attacking midfielder was one of the most skilled players of his generation and played with the Saints from 1986 to 2002 until joining non-league Eastleigh. After retiring, he became a soccer television pundit. Surprisingly, Le Tissier, who was born on the island of Guernsey, played just eight times for England's senior team. Nicknamed "Le God," he was named PFA Young Player of the Year for 1989-90 and was the first midfielder to notch 100 goals in the Premier League. He was tremendous from the 12-yard spot as he netted 47 of 48 penalty kicks for the club. Le Tissier is in the English Football Hall of Fame, was named Southampton Player of the Season three times and to the PFA Premier League Team of the Year for 1994-95.

10. The all-time leading scorer for Southampton is Mick Channon with 228 goals in 607 appearances. He kicked off his career in 1965 and led the top-flight in goals with 21 in 1973-74 but still couldn't help the club avoid relegation that season. The striker helped the side win the 1975-76 FA Cup but then left in 1977 to join top-tier Manchester City. Channon returned to The Dell in 1979 but was

loaned out for stints in 1981 and 1982 before joining Newcastle United permanently. After hanging up his boots, he became an accomplished horse trainer and has a suite named in his honor at St. Mary's Stadium. Channon also tallied 21 goals in 46 games for England.

CONCLUSION

It's been well over 100 years since Southampton FC first took to the soccer pitch under the name of St. Mary's, and you've just re-lived the club's fascinating history since day one. We've tried to serve up the team's story in an entertaining and lighthearted manner by presenting it in trivia form.

We hope you've enjoyed taking a trip down memory lane and hope you may have learned something new during the non-stop journey.

Filled with 12 different chapters and a wealth of "Did You Know?" facts, you should now be well prepared to accept trivia challenges from fellow Saints fans and soccer fans to determine once and for all who's the leader of the pack.

We've included as many of Southampton's top players and managers as possible and provided an informative collection of educational facts and trivia regarding the club's successes, failures, transfers, and records.

We hope you'll feel inclined to share this trivia book with others to help spread the word about the club's captivating history to those who may not be aware of it.

The Southampton story is far from over, and we've told it from the day it started in 1885 right up until April of 2021. We apologize if your favorite club memories and members are absent, but trust you'll be entertained all the same.

Thanks so much for being a loyal and passionate Saints supporter and taking the time to re-live the club's history via our trivia book.